CHRISTMAS PRAYERS AND CUSTOMS

CHRISTMAS CLASSICS

Edited by

Rev. Victor Hoagland, C. P.

Illustrated by

William Luberoff

THE REGINA PRESS
New York

CONTENTS

CELEBRATING CHRISTMAS AND ADVENT

Few times are more sacred for a family or household than Christmas. Along with the Advent Season, Christmas time is rich in traditions which, despite modern commercial exploitation, still stir our hearts and imagination. The Christmas tree, the manger scene, the music and carols, the lights shining in the winter darkness joyfully proclaim the birth of Jesus Christ and call us to come and adore him.

Christmas and Advent can be a spiritual feast for those who live these seasons spiritually. And where better to live them spiritually than in our own homes and households? This book is meant to help families and households celebrate Advent and Christmas in a Christian way.

Christmas and Advent customs appear every where today. True symbols that they are, the living traditions of the season bring peoples and families together and connect us with our ancient faith.

And they respond surprisingly to modern needs as well. The Christmas and Advent seasons uphold so many precious realities presently endangered: birth, children, family, the earth itself. In celebrating Christmas and Advent then, keep their message for today in mind.

In a world where nature and our environment are threatened, let us make our Christmas tree and manger scene reminders of the beauty and sacredness of nature. How closely at his coming did Jesus bind himself to the animals of the field, as well as to the earth and the open sky!

Remembering the poor shepherds and the circumstances of Christ's birth, so marked by poverty, let us make them reminders of the forgotten poor of our world.

Let the Child and Joseph and Mary teach us the dignity and importance of children and families in a society so neglectful of them.

The Christmas season's rich traditions come from peoples throughout the world, from Spain, South America, Eastern Europe, and so many others. Let them remind us of the unity of all people as children of God.

This book may help you celebrate these holy seasons. But use it freely, adding and changing what you will. It's just a starter. May it bring you, your family and friends closer to the mystery you celebrate.

Advent: A Season of Preparation

Begin with Advent, the four weeks before Christmas. It is a time of preparation, waiting and hope. The Advent liturgy resounds with the longing cries of the Hebrew prophets, the voice of Jesus, and John the Baptist's preaching that the Lord is near. Hear their message still ringing through today's dark winters. The brief meditations on the Gospels for the Sundays of Advent found in this section may help you listen to their voices.

Among the customs of Advent, the Advent wreath is probably the most important. Lighting the Advent candles each day with a prayer can prepare your household for Christmas. For children, an Advent calendar marking off the days before Christmas can be an aid for living the season.

And since Santa Claus suddenly appears everywhere at this time, why not remember the saint who is likely his original – St. Nicholas, whose feast day is December 6th? His example of quiet, generous giving is worth recalling, especially for children.

The Advent Wreath

The origins of the Advent wreath are found in the folk practices of the pre-Christian Germanic peoples who, during the cold December darkness of Eastern Europe, gathered wreaths of evergreen and lighted fires as signs of hope in a coming spring and renewed light. Christians kept these popular traditions alive, and by the 16th century Catholics and Protestants throughout Germany used these symbols to celebrate their Advent hope in Christ, the everlasting Light. From Germany the use of the Advent wreath spread to other parts of the Christian world.

Traditionally, the wreath is made of four candles in a circle of evergreens. Three candles are violet and the fourth is rose, but four white or four violet candles can also be used. Each day at home, the candles are lighted, perhaps before the evening meal—one candle the first week, and then another each succeeding week until December 25th. A short prayer may accompany the lighting.

ADVENT WREATH PRAYERS

The Advent wreath appears in church and at home at the beginning of Advent. With four candles placed in a circle of evergreens, the wreath represents the four weeks of Advent before Christmas. The first day the wreath is introduced into the home, the leader may say:

As our nights grow longer and our days grow short, we look on these earthly signs – light and green branches – and remember God's promise to our world: Christ, our Light and our Hope, will come. Listen to the words of Isaiah the prophet:

The people that walked in darkness
    have seen a great light;
    on those who lived
    in a land as dark as death
    a light has dawned.
    You have increased their joy
    and given them great gladness;
    They rejoice in your presence
    as those who rejoice at harvest,
    as warriors exult when dividing spoil.

Is. 9:1-2

Then all pray:

O God,
    rejoicing,
    we remember the promise of your Son.
    As the light from this candle,
    may the blessing of Christ come upon us,
    brightening our way
    and guiding us by his truth.
    May Christ our Savior bring life
    into the darkness of our world,
    and to us, as we wait for his coming.
    We ask this through Christ our Lord.
    Amen.

Then the first candle is lighted.

Each day at home, the candles are lighted, perhaps before the evening meal – one candle the first week, and then another each succeeding week until December 25th. The rose candle is usually lighted on the third Sunday of Advent. As the candles are lighted, the following prayers may be said:

Daily Prayers
For Lighting
The Advent Wreath

First Week

O Emmanuel, Jesus Christ,
    desire of every nation,
    Savior of all peoples,
    come and dwell among us.

Second Week

O King of all nations, Jesus Christ,
    only joy of every heart,
    come and save your people.

Third Week

    O Key of David, Jesus Christ,
the gates of heaven open at your command,
come and let your people free.

Fourth Week

O Wisdom, holy Word of God, Jesus Christ, all
    things are in your hands,
    come and show us the way to salvation.

Come Thou Long Expected Jesus

Come, thou long expected Jesus,
    Born to set thy people free;
    From our fears and sins release us,
    Let us find our rest in thee.

Israel's strength and consolation,
    Hope of all the earth thou art;
    Dear desire of every nation,
    Joy of every longing heart.

Born thy people to deliver,
    Born a child, and yet a king;
    Born to reign in us forever,
    Now thy gracious kingdom bring.

CHARLES WESLEY

ADVENT CHRISTMAS SEASON

"Jesus said to his disciples: 'Be constantly on
the watch! Stay awake!...You do not know
when the Master of the house is coming.'"

MK. 13:33 FIRST SUNDAY OF ADVENT

O Jesus, your voice sounds through the
house of my world: Be on your guard!
Stay awake!

Yet I hardly hear you. Busy with so much,
I go about the things I do like a servant trapped
in household routine, hardly giving a thought
to what my life is about. My spirit within has
grown tired and you, my God, seem far away.
How can I hear your voice today?

Speak to my heart during this season of
grace, as you spoke to your prophets and
saints. Remind me again of the journey you
call me to make and the work you would have
me do. I am your servant, O Lord. Speak to
me in this holy season and turn my eyes to
watch for your coming.

O Emmanuel, Jesus Christ,
desire of every nation, Savior of all peoples,
come and dwell among us.

SECOND WEEK OF ADVENT

When John the Baptizer made his appearance
    as a preacher in the desert of Judea, this
    was his theme: Reform your lives. The
    reign of God is at hand!"

MT. 3:1 SECOND SUNDAY OF ADVENT

O Jesus, in an empty desert your prophet
John proclaimed: God is here, at your side.
God has come to bring about a kingdom
where injustice and suffering will be no more,
where tears will be wiped away, and where
those who turn to God will feast at a banquet.

"Turn now, your God is standing at
your side. Reform your lives, God's kingdom
is at hand." In an empty desert John said
these things.

Give me faith like John's, O Lord, strong
enough to believe even in a desert that you and
your kingdom are no farther from me than my
hand. Make my heart strong like his, not
swayed by trials or snared by false pleasures.
Give me courage to be faithful until your
promises are fulfilled.

O King of all nations, Jesus Christ,
    only joy of every heart,
    come and save your people.

THIRD WEEK OF ADVENT

John's disciples said to Jesus, "Are you 'He
who is to come' or do we look for another?"
In reply Jesus said: "Tell John what you
hear and see: the blind recover their sight,
cripples walk, lepers are cured, and the poor
have good news preached to them…"

LK. 3:10 THIRD WEEK OF ADVENT

O Jesus, I rejoice at the signs that say
you are near. Your power is everywhere if
I could see it.

Yet my eyes often see only darkness and
what has yet to be done. I believe in you,
yet when I look around evil seems so strong
and goodness so weak. If you have come,
why is there still so much suffering and why
do the poor still despair? Where are your
miracles today?

Your grace, O Lord, is more fruitful in
my world than I imagine. I know your power
is everywhere around me, if I could only see
it. Show me today where the blind see and
cripples walk.

Make my vision sharper than it is.

FOURTH WEEK OF ADVENT

The angel Gabriel said to Mary, "Do not fear,
Mary, you shall conceive and bear a son and
give him the name Jesus. Great will be his
dignity and he will be called Son of the
Most High…"

LK. 1 FOURTH SUNDAY OF ADVENT

O Jesus, I believe you were born of Mary
and are God's Son.

Your mysterious coming is beyond
understanding. Yet like your holy mother,
Mary, I wish that you come to me, for you
promised you will. Let me serve you in any
way I can and know that you are with me day
by day as my life goes by.

Like Mary, your mother, though I know
you only by faith, may my whole being proclaim your greatness and my spirit rejoice in
your favor to me.

O Wisdom, holy Word of God, Jesus Christ,
holding all things in your strong yet tender
hands, come and show us the way to
salvation.

St. Nicholas

St. Nicholas, the 4th century saint who inspired our modern figure of Santa Claus, was born near Myra, a port on the Mediterranean Sea serving the busy sea lanes that linked the sea ports of Egypt, Greece and Rome. Ships sailing these waters, laden with grain and all kinds of goods, found safety in the port from raging storms and menacing pirates.

Nicholas came from one of the city's wealthy merchant families, but he was not spoiled by his family's wealth. His mother and father taught him to be generous to others, especially those in need. So Nicholas came to see that helping others makes one richer in life than anything else.

One day, by chance, Nicholas heard about a rich man in Myra who lost all his money when his business failed. The man had three lovely daughters, all wishing to get married, but he had no money for their marriage. Besides, who would marry them, he thought, since their father is such a failure? With nothing to eat, the man in desperation decided to sell one of his daughters into slavery. At least then the rest of them might survive.

The night before the first daughter was to be sold, Nicholas, with a small bag of gold in his hand, softly approached their house, and, tossing the gold through an open window, quickly vanished into the darkness.

The next morning, the father found a bag of gold lying on the floor next to his bed. He had no idea where it came from. "Maybe it's counterfeit," he thought. But as he tested it, he knew it was real. He went over the list of his friends and business associates. None of them could possibly have given him this.

The poor man fell to his knees and great tears came to his eyes. He thanked God for this beautiful gift. His spirits rose higher than they had been for a long time because someone had been so unexpectedly good to him. He arranged for his first daughter's wedding and there was enough money left for the rest of them to live for almost a year. Often he wondered: who gave them the gold?

But by the end of the year, the family again had nothing, and the father, again desperate and seeing no other way open, decided his second daughter must be sold. But Nicholas, hearing about it, came by night to their window and tossed in another bag of gold as before. The next morning the father rejoiced, and, thanking God, begged His pardon for losing hope. Who, though, was the mysterious stranger giving them such a gift?

Each night afterwards the father watched by the window. As the year passed their money ran out. In the dead of one night he heard quiet steps approaching his house and suddenly a bag of gold fell onto the floor. The father quickly ran out to catch the one who threw it there. He caught up with Nicholas some distance away and recognized him, for the young man came from a well-known family in the city.

"Why did you give us the gold?" the father asked.

"Because you needed it," Nicholas answered. "But why didn't you let us know who you were?" the man asked again. "Because it's good to give and have only God know about it."

When the bishop of Myra died, the priests and leading people of the city along with the neighboring bishops came together in their cathedral to select a new bishop. They prayed and asked God to point out who it would be. In a dream, God said to one of them that they should all pray together the next morning. Someone would come through the cathedral door as they prayed. He should be their choice.

It was Nicholas who entered the cathedral the next morning. Immediately, the people of the city named him their bishop, for they knew that this unassuming person, whose good deeds they had learned about, was meant by God to lead them.

As bishop of Myra, Nicholas seemed more aware than ever of people's needs. He would appear all over the city offering help to anyone in difficulty, then quietly disappear without waiting for thanks. He shunned publicity. Still, his reputation as a holy man grew and grew, even spreading to distant cities that had never seen him.

He was especially interested that families had enough to eat and a good place to live, that children got ahead in life, and that old people lived out their lives with dignity and respect. And he always loved the sailors living so dangerously on the sea. Without their ships, people everywhere would be without food and other goods they carried for trade.

Yet, it is as a lover of children that Nicholas is best remembered today. While he lived, he gave the little ones he met small gifts – some candy, a toy. His kindness, which always managed to surprise them, touched their hearts, and they learned from this holy man what a beautiful thing giving is.

In the figure of Santa Claus, whose name and activity Nicholas inspired, we have this saint with us today.

The Christmas Tree

The Christmas tree probably originated from popular early medieval religious plays, "the Paradise Plays," performed in churches and town squares of Europe during the Advent season. The plays told the story of the human race from the creation of Adam and Eve in the Garden of Paradise till the Birth of Jesus in Bethlehem. On stage during the play was a great tree hung with apples, symbolizing the Garden of Paradise. Soon people began the custom of putting a "paradise tree" laden with gifts and lighted with candles in their homes during the Christmas season to celebrate paradise regained through the coming of Christ.

Representing many things – the original tree of paradise, the life-giving tree of Christ's cross, the tree John the Apostle saw in the Book of Revelations, "a tree of life, which yields twelve crops of fruit, one for each month of the year…for the healing of the nations" – our Christmas tree is rich in Christian symbolism.

Prayers Around the Christmas Tree

The leader May begin:

In the beginning God made the world and saw it was good. Long ago, God placed a tree in the garden of paradise as his gift to all human beings, a tree of wisdom and knowledge and laden with every good thing. Our Christmas Tree reminds us of that tree. Long ago too, God's kindness appeared in the coming of Christ, who is our hope of eternal life. This tree is a sign of Christ's blessings.

A reading From the Book of Genesis

This is the story
    of the heavens and the earth
    after their creation.

When the Lord God made
    the earth and the heavens,
    there was neither shrub nor plant
    growing on the earth,
    because the Lord God had sent no rain;
    nor was there anyone to till the ground. . .

The Lord God formed a human being
    from the dust of the ground
    and breathed into his nostrils
    the breath of life,
    so that he became a living creature.

The Lord God planted a garden in Eden
away to the east,
and in it he put the man he had formed...
and in the middle of the garden
he set the tree of life...

GENESIS 2:4-9

Then all pray:

Lord
our God,
the heavens are
the work of your hands,
the moon and the stars you
made;
the earth and the sea, and every
living creature came into being
by your word. And all of us too.
May this tree bring cheer to this house
through Jesus Christ your good and holy Son,
who brings life
and beauty to us
and to our world.
Lighting this tree, we hope in his promise.

*Then the lights of the tree are illuminated and
a carol may be sung.*

Prayers at a Christmas Manger

The leader may say:

It was St. Francis of Assisi who first popularized the Christmas manger. Wanting to see how Christ was born with his own eyes, he had a stable and some images made before Christmas and then invited his neighbors and friends to come and join him at his "Bethlehem. "

As we look on our manger, may the Christmas story unfold before our eyes too.

Listen to the Holy Gospel according to Luke:

In those days a decree was issued
by the emperor Augustus
for a census to be taken
throughout the Roman world.
This was the first registration of its kind;
it took place
when Quirinius was governor of Syria.
Everyone made his way to his own town
to be registered.
Joseph went up to Judaea
from the town of Nazareth in Galilee,
to register
in the city of David called Bethlehem,
because he was of the house of David
by descent;

and with him went Mary, his betrothed,
who was expecting her child.

*(The figures are then placed in the manger,
and after a short period of quiet, the reading
continues)*

While they were there,
    the time came for her to have her baby,
    and she gave birth to a son, her firstborn.
    She wrapped him in swaddling clothes,
    and laid him in a manger,
    because there was no room for them
    in the inn.

LUKE 2:1-7

Then all pray:

O God, whose mighty Son
    was born in Bethlehem
    those days long ago,
    lead us to that same poor place,
    where Mary laid her tiny Child.
    And as we look on in wonder and praise,
    make us welcome him in all new life,
    see him in the poor,
    and care for his handiwork,
    the earth, the sky and the sea.
    O God, bless us again in your great love.
We pray for this through Christ our Lord.
Amen.

A Christmas song may conclude the blessing.

CHRISTMAS CUSTOMS

Centuries ago Christians brought plants and flowers into the celebration of Christmas, for did not Christ come to uphold the dignity of all God's creation?. The natural world, as well as humans, angels and animals, should have a part in welcoming him.

The evergreens, from ancient times symbols of life and eternity, have always had a prominent place in Christian celebrations. Holly, with its green leaves, its prickly points and red berries, suggested that the Child born in the manger would wear a crown of thorns and shed drops of blood. Mistletoe, long associated in the pre-Christian world with healing, became a symbol of the healing power of Christ.

The poinsettia, from Central America, with its bright, starlike flowers, is a natural reminder of the Star of Bethlehem. Other plants that bloom during this season are images also of the Root of David that flowered with new life.

Many nations have contributed a rich mosaic of Christmas customs. Among the Latin peoples, the Christmas novena, nine days of prayer before Christmas, is a popular tradition. The Christmas meal after midnight Mass, in which all the family participates, is traditional among the French. Among the Slavic peoples on Christmas eve, the father of the family breaks the feast day wafers of bread and gives them to the members of his household, while wishing all the peace of Christmas.

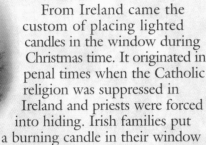

From Ireland came the custom of placing lighted candles in the window during Christmas time. It originated in penal times when the Catholic religion was suppressed in Ireland and priests were forced into hiding. Irish families put a burning candle in their window and left their doors unlatched, hoping that a priest might come to their door and celebrate the Christmas Mass with them.

On the feast of the Epiphany, January 6th, the peoples of South America celebrate the coming of the Three Kings with colorful processions and give gifts on that day.

THE ICON OF THE NATIVITY

Christians of the eastern churches remember the birth of Christ in their centuries-old Icon of the Nativity, which contains so many treasured stories of Christ's birth.

The Infant wrapped in swaddling clothes appears like light in a dark cave surrounded by the mountains and hills of the created world.

"A light shining in the darkness."

JOHN 1:5

His mother Mary turns her face and invites us to share her great secret. An ox and an ass keep him company.

Is. I :3

The heavenly world proclaims the Child as angels minister to him and announce his birth to the shepherds. And a star points him out to the wise men coming from the east. He has come for the poor and the rich, the humble and the wise.

Joseph appears at the bottom of the icon, pondering the mystery. Two women bathe the newborn child as a sign that he is truly human.

Prayers for the New Year

The leader may begin:

The new year, like a new born child, is placed in our hands as the old year passes away. The days and weeks to come are God's gift; they carry God's blessing. As a blessing we welcome them. Our hope for the year ending is that all that was good in it remain with us and all that was harmful be left behind.

Listen to a Reading from the Book of Genesis:

In the beginning
God created the heavens and the earth.
The earth was a vast waste,
darkness covered the deep,
and the spirit of God
hovered over the surface of the water.
God said: "Let there be light,"
and there was light;
and God saw the light was good,
and he separated the light from darkness.
He called the light day,
and the darkness night.
So evening came, and morning came;
it was the first day.

GENESIS 1:1-5

Then all pray

Bless us, O Lord;
  and bless the time and seasons
  yet to come.
  Teach us to number our days aright,
  that we may gain wisdom of heart.
  And fill this new year with your kindness,
  that we may be glad and rejoice
  all the days of our life.
  Others may offer prayers of intercession
and thanksgiving, and then all may pray the
'Our Father.'
  Since January 1st is a day for praying for
peace, the Prayer of St. Francis may also be said.

Lord, make me an instrument of your peace:
  where there is hatred, let me sow love;
  where there is injury, pardon;
  where there is doubt, faith;
  where there is despair, hope;
  where there is darkness, light;
  where there is sadness, joy.

Good Master, grant
  that I may not so much seek to be con-
  soled
  as to console,
  to be understood as to understand,
  to be loved as to love.
  For it is in giving that we receive,
  it is in pardoning that we are pardoned,
  it is in dying
  that we are born to eternal life. Amen.

Prayers for a Home

During the Christmas season, the feast of the Epiphany is an appropriate day for praying for a home.

As the household gathers around the manger, the leader may begin:

On this day we remember the Magi who, guided by the star shining in the heavens, came to the house where Jesus rested in the arms of Mary his mother. They were blessed as they brought their gifts to that holy place. Today we ask Christ our Lord to bless our home and make it his dwelling.

Listen to the holy Gospel according to John:

In the beginning the Word already was.

The Word was in God's presence,
  and what God was, the Word was.

He was with God in the beginning,
　without him no created thing
　came into being.
　So the Word became flesh;
　he made his home among us,
　and we saw his glory,
　such glory as befits the Father's only Son,
　full of grace and truth.

JOHN 1:1-3, 14.

*Intercessions by household members for various
needs are made.
　Then all say the following prayer:*

O God,
　by your heavenly star,
　you guided those who were wise
　to your beloved Son, Jesus Christ.

May your blessing come to rest
　on our home and all of us.
　Make our lives wise with your wisdom,
　true to your teaching,
　and enlivened by your love.
　May your Word made flesh
　make his home among us. Amen.

Prayers for a Family

The Feast of the Holy Family, the Sunday following Christmas, is an appropriate day for prayers for a family. The leader may begin:

From the beginning, God joined man and woman together, and blessing them with children, made them a family. Just as Jesus lived at Nazareth with Mary and Joseph and his relatives and friends, so we find our life here with our own flesh and blood. We ask God's blessing on our family and our home.

Listen to the words of Paul the Apostle to the Colossians:

Put on, then, garments that suit
    God's chosen and beloved people:
    compassion, kindness,
    humility, gentleness, patience.
Be tolerant with one another and forgiving,
    if any of you has cause for complaint:
    you must forgive as the Lord forgave you.

Finally, to bind everything together
and complete the whole,
there must be love.
Let Christ's peace be arbiter
in your decisions,
the peace to which you were called
as members of a single body.
Always be thankful.
Let the gospel of Christ dwell among you
in all its richness;
teach and instruct one another
with all the wisdom it gives you.

COLOSSIANS 3:12-16

After some moments of silence, prayers for the family may be offered, especially for those members who have died. Then all say:

O God,
bless our family
and all its members and friends;
bind us together by your love.
Give us kindness and patience
to support each other;
and wisdom in all we do.
Let the gift of your peace
come into our hearts,
and remain with us.
May we rejoice in your blessings
for all our days.
Amen.

SONGS AND CAROLS

O Come, O Come, Emmanuel

O Come, O Come, Emmanuel,
    And ransom captive Israel,
    That mourns in lonely exile here
    Until the Son of God appear.

Rejoice Rejoice! O Israel
    To thee shall come Emmanuel!
    O come, thou wisdom, from on high,
    And order all things far and nigh;
    To us the path of knowledge show,
    And teach us in her ways to go.

Rejoice! Rejoice! O Israel
    To thee shall come Emmanuel!

THOMAS HELMORE

O Come, All Ye Faithful

O come, all ye faithful,
 Joyful and triumphant
  O come ye, o come ye, to Bethlehem;
 Come and behold him,
 Born the King of angels.

Chorus:
O come, let us adore him,
 O come, let us adore him,
 O come, let us adore him,
 Christ the Lord.

Sing choirs of angels,
 Sing in exultation,
  Sing all ye citizens of heav'n above:
 Glory to God
 In the highest!

Yea, Lord, we greet Thee
 Born this happy morning
 Jesus, to Thee be glory giv'n
 Word of the Father
 Now in flesh appearing

JOHN FRANCIS WADE

Silent Night

Silent night, Holy night!
    All is calm, all is bright
    'Round yon Virgin Mother and Child,
    Holy Infant so tender and mild,
    Sleep in heavenly peace,
    Sleep in heavenly peace!

Silent night, Holy night!
    Shepherds quake at the sight!
    Glories stream from heaven afar,
    Heav'nly hosts sing Alleluia;
    Christ the Savior is born,
    Christ the Savior is born!

Silent night, Holy night!
    Son of God, love's pure light,
    Radiant beams from Thy holy face,
    With the dawn of redeeming grace,
    Jesus, Lord, at Thy birth,
    Jesus, Lord, at Thy birth.

JOSEPH MOHR

Away In A Manger

Away in a manger, no crib for his bed,
The little Lord Jesus
laid down his sweet head;
The stars in the bright sky,
looked down where he lay,
The little Lord Jesus, asleep on the hay.

The cattle are lowing, the baby awakes,
But little Lord Jesus, no crying he makes,
I love you, Lord Jesus;
Look down from on high,
And stay by my side
Until morning is nigh.

Be near me, Lord Jesus, I ask you to stay
Close by me forever, and love me, I pray;
Bless all the dear children
in your tender care,
And fit us for heaven,
to live with you there.

ANONYMOUS

The First Noel

The first Noel the angel did say
    Was to certain poor shepherds
    In fields as they lay;
    In fields where they lay keeping their sheep
    On a cold winter's night that was so deep.
    Noel, Noel, Noel, Noel,
    Born is the King of Israel.

They looked up and saw a star
    Shining in the east, beyond them far,
    And to the earth it gave great light,
    And so it continued both day and night.
    Noel, Noel, Noel, Noel,
    Born is the King of Israel.

This star drew nigh to the northwest,
    O'er Bethlehem it took its rest,
    And there it did both stop and stay
    Right over the place where Jesus lay.
    Noel, Noel, Noel, Noel,
    Born is the King of Israel.

Now let us all with one accord
    Sing praises to our heavenly Lord,
    Who brought forth heaven
    and earth from nought,
    And with his blood humankind has bought.

ANONYMOUS

O little town of Bethlehem

O little town of Bethlehem,
    How still we see thee lie,
    Above thy deep and dreamless sleep
    The silent stars go by;
    Yet in thy dark streets shineth
    The everlasting light,
    The hopes and fears of all the years
    Are met in thee tonight.

For Christ is born of Mary,
    And gathered all above,
    While mortals sleep, the angels keep
    Their watch of wond'ring love.
    O morning stars, together
    Proclaim the holy birth,
    And praises sing to God the King,
    And peace to men on earth.

O holy Child of Bethlehem,
    Descend on us we pray;
    Cast out our sin and enter in,
    Be born in us today.
    We hear the Christmas angels
    The great, glad tidings tell;
    O come to us, abide with us,
    Our Lord Emmanuel.

PHILLIPS BROOKS

Hark! The Herald Angels Sing,

Hark! the herald angels sing,
    Glory to the newborn King!
    Peace on earth and mercy mild,
    God and sinners reconciled!
    Joyful all ye nations rise,
    Join the triumph of the skies;
    With th' angelic host proclaim,
    Christ is born in Bethlehem.
    Hark the herald angels sing
    Glory to the newborn King!

Christ, by highest heaven adored,
    Christ, the everlasting Lord,
    Late in time behold Him come,
    Offspring of a virgin's womb!
    Veiled in flesh, the Godhead see;
    Hail th' Incarnate Deity!
    Pleased as man with man to dwell
    Jesus, our Emmanuel.

CHARLES WESLEY

What Child Is This

What child is this, who, laid to rest,
    On Mary's lap is sleeping?
    Whom angels greet with anthems sweet,
    While shepherds watch are keeping?
    This, this is Christ the King.
    Whom shepherds guard and angels sing;
    Haste, haste to bring him laud,
    The Babe, the Son of Mary.

Why lies he in such mean estate,
    Where ox and ass are feeding?
    Good Christian, fear, for sinners here
    The silent Word is pleading.
    Nails, spear, shall pierce him through,
    The cross he bore for me, for you;
    Hail, hail, the Word made flesh,
    The Babe, the Son of Mary!

So bring him incense, gold and myrrh,
    Come, peasant, king, to own him;
    The King of Kings salvation brings,
    Let loving hearts enthrone him.
    Raise, raise the song on high,
    The virgin sings her lullaby;
    Joy, joy, for Christ is born,
    The Babe, the Son of Mary!

WILLIAM CHATTERTON DIX

Go Tell It On The Mountain

Refrain:
Go tell it on the mountain
　　Over the hills and everywhere,
　　Go tell it on the mountain,
　　Our Jesus Christ is born.

When I was a learner,
　　I sought both night and day;
　　I asked the Lord to help me,
　　And he showed me the way.

(Refrain)

While shepherds kept their watching
　　O'er wand'ring flocks at night;
　　Behold from out the heavens
　　There came a holy night.

(Refrain)

Lo, when they had seen it,
　　They all bowed down and prayed;
　　They traveled on together
　　To where the babe was laid.

(Refrain)

ANONYMOUS

Joy to the World!

Joy to the world! the Lord is come;
  Let earth receive her King;

Let every heart Prepare Him room,
  And heav'n and nature sing,
  And heav'n and nature sing,
  And heav'n, and heav'n and nature sing.

Joy to the earth! the Savior reigns;
  Let men their songs employ;
  While fields and floods
  Rocks, hills and plains,
  Repeat the sounding joy,
  Repeat the sounding joy,
  Repeat, repeat the sounding joy.

He rules the world! with truth and grace;
  And makes the nations prove
  The glories of
  His righteousness
  And wonders of His love,
  And wonders of His love,
  And wonders, wonders of His love.

ISAAC WATTS

POEMS AND PRAYERS

In The Bleak Mid-Winter

In the bleak mid-winter
    Frosty wind made moan,
    Each stood hard as iron,
    Water like a stone;
    Snow had fallen, snow on snow,
    Snow on snow, In the bleak mid-winter
    Long ago.

Our God, heaven cannot hold him,
    Nor earth sustain;
    Heaven and earth shall flee away
    When he comes to reign:
    In the bleak mid-winter
    A stable-place sufficed
    The Lord God Almighty
    Jesus Christ.

Enough for him, whom cherubim
    Worship night and day,
    A breastful of milk
    And a mangerful of hay;
    Enough for him, whom angels
    Fall down before,
    The ox and ass and camel
    Which adore.

Angels and archangels
    May have gathered there;
    Cherubim and seraphim
    Thronged the air;
    But only his Mother
    In her maiden bliss
    Worshiped the beloved
    With a kiss.

What can I give him,
    Poor as I am?
    If I were a shepherd
    I would bring him a lamb,
    If I were a wise man
    I would do my part,
    Yet what can I give him,
    Give my heart.

CHRISTINA ROSSETTI

The Nativity of Christ

Behold the father is his daughter's son,
    The bird that built the nest
    is hatched therein,
    The old of years an hour hath not outrun,
    Eternal life to live doth now begin,
    The Word is dumb,
    the mirth of heaven doth weep,
    Might feeble is,
    and force doth faintly creep.

O dying souls, behold your living spring;
    O dazzled eyes, behold your sun of grace;
    Dull ears,
    attend what word this Word doth bring;
    Up, heavy hearts, with joy your joy
    embrace.
    From death, from dark,
    from deafness, from despair:
    This life, this light,
    his Word, this joy repairs.

Gift better than himself God doth not know;
    Gift better than his God no man can see.
    This gift doth here the giver given bestow;
    Gift to this gift let each receiver be.
    God is my gift, himself he freely gave me;
    God's gift am I,
    and none but God shall have me.

Man altered was by sin from man to beast;
  Beast's food is hay, hay is all mortal flesh.
  Now God is flesh and lies in manger pressed
  As hay, the brutest sinner to refresh.
  O happy field wherein this fodder grew,
  Whose taste doth from beasts to men renew.

ROBERT SOUTHWELL

A Christmas Prayer

O God our loving Father, help us
    rightly to remember the birth of Jesus,
    that we may share in the song of the angels,
    the gladness of the shepherds
    and the worship of the wise men.

Close the door of hate
    and open the door of love all over the world.

Deliver us from evil
    by the blessing that Christ brings,
    and teach us to be merry with clear hearts.

May the Christmas morning make us
    happy to be your children,
    and the Christmas evening
    bring us to our beds with grateful thoughts,
    forgiving and forgiven,
    for Jesus' sake. Amen.

ROBERT LOUIS STEVENSON